THE FIRST SONGS OF CHRISTMAS

MEDITATIONS ON LUKE 1 & 2

A 31-DAY ADVENT DEVOTIONAL

NANCY DEMOSS WOLGEMUTH

To the generous friends
whose partnership in the ministry of
Revive Our Hearts
is causing many to sing
new songs of praise
to Christ, our Savior and King

CONTENTS

Call to Worship   10

Elizabeth's Song: "The Beatitude"   15

Mary's Song: "The Magnificat"   32

Zechariah's Song: "The Benedictus"   62

The Angels' Song: "Gloria!"   97

Simeon's Song: "The Nunc Dimittis"   119

Hymn of Response   140

INTRODUCTION

ne of the things I most love about being a child of God is that we have something to sing about. And one of the things I most love about the Bible is that it gives us songs to sing.

Especially Christmas songs.

Had you noticed? The very first songs of the very first Christmas are some of the very first words of the New Testament. Six of these songs (depending how you count them) are recorded in the first two chapters of Luke's gospel.

- *Elizabeth's Song*—the joy of an older woman, relieved of her barrenness, yet caught up in the thrill of another woman's even more amazing pregnancy

- *Mary's Song*—a biblically rich lyric, expressed by a teenage girl losing her fear of the unknown, overshadowed by her awe for a God who knew where to find her

- *Zechariah's Song*—twelve monumental verses, sung with the reverence of an elderly priest, but also the fervor of one whose tongue had just come unloosed

- *The Angels' Song*—two songs really, each sung to the shepherds: one in the clear voice of a lone angel; the second from an angel chorus in unified worship

- *Simeon's Song*—the benedictory prayer of a watchful saint attuned to God's timing, aware that he was seeing in Jesus the gospel's grand mystery in miniature

These five (or six) songs, the original songs of Christmas, are different from many of the ones that get the majority of airplay this time of year. They're not self-centered; they're God-centered. They speak less to what Christmas does for us, and more to what Christmas reveals about the greatness, glory, and goodness of God. Rather than being clever rhymes filled with memories and nostalgia, they are biblical lines of historic verse about His redemptive plan for the world and His eternal purpose for the ages.

In other words, they create an ideal template for experiencing Advent—Christ's coming into the world, God becoming flesh. What else could capture so vividly, delivered fresh from that moment, the outburst of joy erupting in God's people as slowly, yet suddenly, streaks of heavenly light began appearing in their darkness? After years, decades, centuries of oppression and hardship—wondering if God had forgotten them forever—those who'd kept watching experienced something in person that we still can't stop singing about today.

They not only have stories to tell; they have songs to sing. And this year, I'd love for us to sing them together.

Each day in this book revolves around a single line from one of these songs. In addition to a brief devotional thought, I've also included a few other things you can consider doing if your time and situation allow—other Bible passages to look up and learn from, a journaling question to contemplate. The goal is not to check through the items, making sure you complete everything. I only pray, however many of these days you're able to spend in these pages throughout the entire month leading up to and beyond Christmas, you'll spend them lifting up your eyes the way each of these men and women did, your face fully fixed on our great God and Savior.

Our Christmas song.

Nancy

NEVER IMPOSSIBLE

"The Holy Spirit will come upon you, and the power of the Most High will overshadow you; therefore the child to be born will be called holy—the Son of God. . . . For nothing will be impossible with God."
(Luke 1:35, 37)

he Ancient of Days became a newborn. The One who created the first woman was born of a woman.

Though heaven and earth cannot contain Him, He chose to be confined to a human body. He chose to be held in the arms of a teenage girl, even though His own arms, His "everlasting arms" (Deut. 33:27), hold the entire universe in place. He whose voice is "powerful" and "full of majesty" (Ps. 29:4) was reduced to "speaking" with the coo and cry of a tiny baby. He who "sits enthroned over the flood; the LORD [who] sits enthroned as king forever" (Ps. 29:10) exchanged His lofty throne for an animal's feeding trough.

Impossible.

Yet in this case, because the story of Jesus' birth is so known and familiar to us, we do something we don't do often enough. *We believe the impossible.* We sing with joyful acceptance about things that make no earthly sense unless God actually did what cannot possibly be done. We marvel at it, and we worship Him for it, despite our inability to understand it. Because since it's baby Jesus, since it's the Christmas story . . . it doesn't sound so impossible anymore.

This year, however, as you prepare for Christmas, don't start with what you already know of the story. Imagine yourself instead in the heart of a young girl to whom the events of Luke 1 occurred on just another ordinary day, in a place where impossible things never happened. She didn't wake up that morning expecting an angel to visit. She had no way of knowing ahead of time what God had chosen her to do, much less how He intended to do it. She was likely thinking of little else besides her plans for getting married and living happily into the future with her future husband. She held in her mind, as perhaps you hold in yours, a simple little picture of what her life was to be like—a picture framed by nothing but *possible* outcomes.

Yet before her name became written in Scripture, before her likeness was carved and colored into countless nativity scenes—before Christmas became somehow easy for us to believe—

Mary believed. She believed the impossible.

"For nothing will be impossible with God."

Surely in this December season, you're faced with God-assigned tasks where you're asking, "How can I do this? I don't have the ability. I don't have the time. I don't have the resources. *This is impossible!*" But your task, like Mary's task, is meant to be made possible only by the power of the Holy Spirit. You and I must be willing to surrender ourselves by faith and let God take over, knowing He alone can do the impossible through us.

MY PRAYER

Lord, apart from You, I will accomplish nothing of eternal significance today or throughout this Christmas season. So I look to You to overshadow me, to fill me with Your Spirit, and enable me to accomplish all You have purposed for me to do. Help me not trust in my own strengths, skills, or success, but only in You, for Your honor and glory alone.

KEEP READING

— Deuteronomy 33:26–29
"Who is like you, a people saved by the LORD!" (v. 29)

— Psalm 29:1–11
"May the LORD give strength to his people" (v. 11)

— John 15:1–8
"For apart from me you can do nothing" (v. 5)

MY RESPONSE

Even if the tasks awaiting you in the coming days are things you've done many times before, how might they grow in significance as you consciously depend on God to perform them?

ELIZABETH'S SONG
"THE BEATITUDE"

In those days Mary arose and went with haste
into the hill country, to a town in Judah,
and she entered the house of Zechariah and greeted Elizabeth.
And when Elizabeth heard the greeting of Mary,
the baby leaped in her womb.

And Elizabeth was filled with the Holy Spirit,
and she exclaimed with a loud cry,

"Blessed are you among women,
and blessed is the fruit of your womb!
And why is this granted to me
that the mother of my Lord should come to me?
For behold, when the sound of your greeting came to my ears,
the baby in my womb leaped for joy.
And blessed is she who believed
that there would be a fulfillment
of what was spoken to her from the Lord."

(Luke 1:39–45)

WHERE THE SONG COMES FROM

When Elizabeth heard the greeting of Mary, the baby leaped in her womb. And Elizabeth was filled with the Holy Spirit, and she exclaimed with a loud cry, "Blessed are you among women, and blessed is the fruit of your womb!"
(Luke 1:41–42)

Long before Christmas actually arrives, it is already on everyone's tongue. You hear its music in the shops and stores; you see its lights and colors in people's windows. Even during random encounters with others, where ordinarily you might not know what to say, "Merry Christmas" is the season's universal catchphrase. Everyone understands it and generally expects it.

But when Elizabeth opened her door to Mary, who had just arrived from Nazareth, customary greetings went out the window. Instead she cried out, "Blessed are you!"—the Greek word which is translated "blessed" is the word from which we get our English word *eulogy*, referring to the gracious, complimentary things we typically say of people at their death. It means "to speak well of, to express good wishes."

"Blessed are you!" Elizabeth exclaimed. This is why her song, which begins in Luke 1:42 and covers four total verses, is traditionally known as the *Beatitude*, conveying words of "supreme blessedness or happiness."

But notice: happiness is not what motivated her to burst into blessing at the sight of Mary's appearing, though Elizabeth did have good reason to be happy. Only recently, she had been a childless woman, past child-bearing age, but God had answered her lifelong prayer. In the months leading up to this visit from Mary, He had miraculously enabled her to conceive.

And yet the words of blessing she spoke came not from being filled with happiness but from being "filled with the Holy Spirit." She was not only a woman who was "righteous before God," who walked "blamelessly in all the commandments and statutes of the Lord" (Luke 1:6); she was also willing to be controlled and guided by God's Spirit. And *that's* where her blessing came from—because she actually had no way of knowing Mary's news, except that the Spirit had given her revelation. He provided her both the insight and incentive to bless Mary in a way that celebrated what her young relative was experiencing.

God has placed His Spirit inside His children to lead us, to counsel us, and—yes, even to show us what to say. His presence should affect the way we talk. Filled with the Holy Spirit, our mouths should be filled with words like those of Elizabeth, words that are gracious and life-giving ("Blessed are you among women"), words that express our praise and worship ("and blessed is the fruit of your womb").

Too often, we speak before we're consciously aware of the Holy Spirit's direction and discernment about what to say. May we learn, as Elizabeth did, the importance of letting our tongues be guided by Him. This Christmas, ask Him to employ your words so that they bless those around you, saying not just what comes mechanically to mind but what God Himself has given you to tell them.

MY PRAYER

Father, thank You for the opportunities You give each day to speak blessing into others' lives. Help me to see my words as a stewardship— not a possession to use as I want, but a gift to be shared at Your prompting and pleasure. May my speech always give evidence that Your Spirit truly resides within me, so that people feel Your touch when they hear my voice.

———————◆———————

KEEP READING

— Psalm 85:8–9
"Let me hear what God the LORD will speak" (v. 8)

— Proverbs 2:1–6
"From his mouth come knowledge and understanding" (v. 6)

— Ephesians 5:15–21
"addressing one another in psalms and hymns and spiritual songs" (v. 19)

———————◆———————

MY RESPONSE

How would you assess the weight and impact of most of your conversations? Think of deliberate ways you could elevate them this Christmas—in value, in blessing, in God-honoring tone.

OUTWARD AND UPWARD

*"And why is this granted to me that the mother of
my Lord should come to me?"*
(Luke 1:43)

lizabeth had so much to talk about. Imagine the stories and testimony an older woman in her situation could tell. It had been an unbelievable six months since the angelic announcement concerning her pregnancy, yet she'd spent most of that time in seclusion, keeping everything to herself. And with her husband unable to communicate, having been struck dumb by the angel for his disbelief, the sudden sight of Mary at the door must have felt like—finally, an audience! Someone she could talk to!

But see where Elizabeth focused her attention instead.

Not on herself, but on Mary. I love the picture here of an older woman ministering to a younger woman. Rather than assuming that her age, status, and experience made her the most important participant in this relationship, Elizabeth humbled herself. She recognized that God was doing something special in Mary's life, and she placed first priority on making sure she met the needs of her guest above her own.

I can remember my dad saying when I was a girl, "When you're with other people, ask them questions about themselves." Not only is this an acknowledgment that people are usually more interested in talking about their own lives than ours, it's really just a demonstration of love. Love is concerned about the other person first. Love focuses outward.

Elizabeth seemed to understand at once that Mary needed some love here, some reassurance, some encouragement. Mary needed someone else to believe with her what God had told her. She needed what all of us need from our mentors—words that stimulate faith in our hearts, words that affirm us in our obedience and help banish our fears.

When you begin to desire more from your life's pilgrimage than merely personal blessings, He will open doors of ministry to others who are going through similar circumstances and situations. Elizabeth focused not on herself, but on Mary. And . . .

Not on herself, but on Christ. "Why is this granted to me that the mother of my Lord should come to me?" This baby in Mary's womb was not just anyone; He was (and is) Christ the Lord. And not only is He the Lord—Elizabeth proclaimed Him to be *her* Lord, the object of her personal worship and devotion.

Elizabeth's song (like Mary's song, which we'll soon consider) was supremely focused on God and His character. These two women, as remarkable as their lives were turning out to be, were not the point of the events taking place. Jesus was the center of the story. And so should He be in our story, and in all our interactions with others.

Not on herself, but on Mary.
Not on herself, but on Christ.
May our lives reflect a similar focus.

MY PRAYER

Thank You, Father, for making Your Son the ultimate example of humility. When I look to Him, may Your Spirit quench my pride, causing me to pour myself out in care for others—and in worship of You. Keep me ever sensitive to the needs around me, and multiply what You have already invested in my life, so that You will be praised.

KEEP READING

— Ruth 2:8–13
"Why have I found favor in your eyes?" (v. 10)

— Psalm 69:30–33
"When the humble see it they will be glad" (v. 32)

— Philippians 2:1–4
"In humility count others more significant than yourselves" (v. 3)

MY RESPONSE

"Death and life," the Bible says, "are in the power of the tongue" (Proverbs 18:21). Whose life might God be directing you toward this Christmas season to provide encouragement and support?

PRAISE IS DUE

"Behold, when the sound of your greeting came to my ears, the baby in my womb leaped for joy."
(Luke 1:44)

Christmas, I realize, can whip itself up into a whirlwind of activities and get-togethers, of food to be baked and presents to be bought. Church becomes busy, family life is busy, friends are busy, the airports and highways are busy. And you may find that in the busyness—having done all these things for so many years as part of celebrating the holiday—you've lost some of the sense of wonder and worship at what Christmas is all about.

This is why we need to spend today in this verse, Luke 1:44, this little private moment that God preserved for us in Scripture, where a tiny baby *in utero* "leaped" when he found himself in close proximity to God incarnate.

The leaping that Elizabeth felt in her womb is the same word used in the Old Testament to describe Jacob and Esau struggling together in the womb of their mother Rebekah (Gen. 25:22). But in Psalm 114:3–4, its usage is even more descriptive of the intensity of this word, where the writer captured the joy of Israel's release from Egypt.

> *The sea looked and fled;*
> *Jordan turned back.*
> *The mountains skipped like rams,*
> *the hills like lambs.*

Skipping, leaping—that's what a pregnant girl's arrival at Elizabeth's home made the older woman's yet unborn son, John the Baptist, feel like doing.

He "leaped for joy"—joy because of what God was doing to bring about the redemption of His people. Darkness was turning to light. Death was being brought to life. Despair was being turned into hope. After four hundred years of silence, the voice of God would finally be heard again. The great and glorious God, before whom angels covered their faces, was coming to earth as a Man. "The Word became flesh and dwelt among us, and we have seen his glory, glory as of the only Son from the Father, full of grace and truth" (John 1:14).

That's something to leap for joy about!

> *Joy to the world! the Lord is come;*
> *Let earth receive her King;*
> *Let every heart prepare Him room,*
> *And heaven and nature sing.*

Your temperament may or may not be one that naturally lends itself to ecstatic, spontaneous expressions of excitement. But if we pause to contemplate what all this frantic, holiday motion of ours is supposed to be celebrating, should joy not well up in each of our hearts at what God did for the world that first Christmas?

The angel had said to Zechariah, in reference to the birth of John, "You will have joy and gladness, and many will rejoice at his birth" (Luke 1:14). But John would later say of Jesus, "He who is coming after me is mightier than I, whose sandals I am not worthy to carry" (Matt. 3:11). The real birth, the great birth, is the birth of Jesus Christ.

Leap for joy.

MY PRAYER

Lord, restore to me the joy of my salvation. How can I not be more excited at the demonstration of Your extreme love for sinners (like me) than at anything else that feels important about my day? Forgive me for crowding from my mind the worship I owe You for becoming one of us at such a great cost. Hear and receive my heartfelt worship this day.

KEEP READING

— Psalm 98:4–9
"Let the rivers clap their hands; let the hills sing for joy together" (v. 8)

— Isaiah 35:3–7
"Then shall the lame man leap like a deer" (v. 6)

— Galatians 4:4–7
"When the fullness of time had come, God sent forth his Son" (v. 4)

MY RESPONSE

What changes could you make, whether in activity or approach, that could make this Christmas a season of greater wonder, awe, gratitude, and worship—real joy—at what Jesus has done?

UNEXPECTED BLESSING

"Blessed is she who believed that there would be a fulfillment of what was spoken to her from the Lord."
(Luke 1:45)

lizabeth's song—the *Beatitude*—is a touching and tender, yet powerful, testament to the vital importance of having fellowship with like-minded believers. We are not intended to be self-sufficient. We need each other. We need to spend time with people who have a thriving relationship with God if we expect to be strong in our own faith and to strengthen them in theirs.

Mary *needed* this blessing that Elizabeth spoke over her. She *needed* what the Spirit was saying to her through her dear friend and older cousin.

Here's why I'm so sure of it. The word translated "blessed" in

Luke 1:45 is a different word than the "blessed" of verse 42, the one that equates to *eulogy*. This one ("Blessed is she who believed") is the Greek word *makarios*, meaning, "one whom God makes fully satisfied"—not because of favorable circumstances, but because God Himself provides the satisfaction. To be *makarios* is to be fully content, even in situations that are less than ideal, solely because God lives in us through Christ.

It's the state of being *saved*, in other words. No matter what we are called to endure as Christians, we have all we need . . . because we have Jesus.

Mary was arguably in the most difficult circumstance a young woman could imagine. Think about what she had to be willing to embrace if she were to say yes to the plan of God in her life. She had to be willing to become pregnant under a cloud of mystery, willing to carry the child to term, and willing to endure the inevitable misunderstanding and ridicule that came from her unique situation. She had no verifiable way of refuting others' claims that she'd been either unfaithful to Joseph or involved immorally with him. In addition, according to the Old Testament law, she could possibly be subject to stoning for this alleged offense. What she was really saying, then, by surrendering to God's purpose was, "I am willing to give up my life to do what He says."

To this woman, Elizabeth said, "*Blessed is she who believed that there would be a fulfillment of what was spoken to her from the Lord.*" To this woman, Elizabeth said that God would bless her with full satisfaction in Him if she would believe what He had promised.

How much do you think Mary needed to hear that?

As do we . . . because you and I will never be happy if we are not believing the promises of God. Joy and blessing, satisfaction and fullness, come from one source alone. They are the byproduct of believing what God has said. And they are the blessings we can encourage in our brothers and sisters by committing ourselves to each other through Christ.

MY PRAYER

Father, I praise You for the salvation You have given us by grace through faith in Your Son Jesus Christ. I praise You, too, not only for meeting our great eternal need but also blessing us with access to peace, joy, contentment—complete satisfaction in You, despite every struggle. Help us cling to this hope as You cause us to experience it, both individually and together.

KEEP READING

— Psalm 16:7–11
"Because he is at my right hand, I shall not be shaken" (v. 8)

— Habakkuk 3:17–19
"I will take joy in the God of my salvation" (v. 18)

— 1 Peter 1:3–8
"joy that is inexpressible and full of glory" (v. 8)

MY RESPONSE

At what level are you currently experiencing Christian fellowship with other believers? If you're struggling with a shortage of it, how could you initiate a greater depth of relationship?

MARY'S SONG
"THE MAGNIFICAT"

And Mary said,

"My soul magnifies the Lord,
and my spirit rejoices in God my Savior,
for he has looked on the humble estate of his servant.
For behold, from now on all generations will call me blessed;
for he who is mighty has done great things for me,
and holy is his name.
And his mercy is for those who fear him
from generation to generation.

"He has shown strength with his arm;
he has scattered the proud in the thoughts of their hearts;
he has brought down the mighty from their thrones
and exalted those of humble estate;
he has filled the hungry with good things,
and the rich he has sent away empty.
He has helped his servant Israel,
in remembrance of his mercy,
as he spoke to our fathers,
to Abraham and to his offspring forever."

(Luke 1:46–55)

WORD IN, WORD OUT

Mary said, "My soul magnifies the Lord, and my spirit rejoices in God my Savior."
(Luke 1:46–47)

Probably the most well-known piece of information about Mary's song of praise in Luke 1 (verses 46–55) is its given name, the title that has been ascribed to it throughout history: the *Magnificat*. Simply stated, *Magnificat* is the first word of her prayer in the Latin translation. And as beautiful a word as it sounds all by itself, the song in its entirety is perhaps one of the most beautiful passages in all the Bible.

It's similar in ways to two songs from the Old Testament which were also sung and/or prayed by women. The first is Miriam's song (Ex. 15:21), sung with tambourine and dance on the saved side of the Red Sea, commemorating God's deliverance of His people from the Egyptian armies. The second, which contains even more similarities to the *Magnificat*, is the song of Hannah (1 Sam. 2:1–10). The mother of Samuel offered this praise for the gift of her son, whom she gave back to the Lord, allowing him to serve with Eli the priest in the house of God.

The remarkable thing is that Mary, though young, uneducated, and likely illiterate, must have known these songs well. In fact, in the few lines that make up the song of Mary, as many as fifteen Old Testament quotes or allusions appear. The opening stanza itself—"*My soul magnifies the Lord, and my spirit rejoices in God my Savior*"—roughly mirrors the words of Hannah, and sounds quite close to some of the language we hear from David:

> *Oh, magnify the Lord with me,*
> *and let us exalt his name together!* (Ps. 34:3)

> *Bless the Lord, O my soul,*
> *and all that is within me,*
> *bless his holy name!* (Ps. 103:1)

Basically, then, we see that Mary, despite her lack of formal schooling, despite not having a copy of the Hebrew Scriptures lying around the house—certainly not in every color and size and translation and binding—was a young woman of the Word. She was familiar with it. She'd been exposed to it. Apparently, she'd heard it often at synagogue when she'd gone there to worship.

But more than just hearing it, she'd internalized it. She had listened to it. She had grown familiar with it. She had retained it.

She loved it . . . so that when she opened her mouth to speak, when she went to the Lord in prayer and praise, what came out was the Word of God.

If we are going to be used of Him in our generation, we too must saturate our hearts and minds in the Scripture. We must know it, live it, breathe it, speak it. We must be lifelong people of His Word.

MY PRAYER

Lord, thank You for giving us Your Word, for revealing Yourself to us not only in creation but also in writing. Thank You for not leaving us here to guess what You're like, lost in trying to discern truth from error. Help me not squander this gift—the Bible—but rather run to it, stay in it, and absorb it as Your Spirit opens my eyes to understand. Make me a person of Your Word.

———————◆———————

KEEP READING

— Deuteronomy 32:44–47
"It is no empty word for you, but your very life" (v. 47)

— Psalm 119:33–40
"Incline my heart to your testimonies" (v. 36)

— 2 Timothy 3:14–17
"Continue in what you have learned and have firmly believed" (v. 14)

———————◆———————

MY RESPONSE

Consider meditating on this song of Mary throughout the day as you continue preparing your heart for Christmas. What does this first line alone tell you as you prayerfully ponder it?

WHY ME?

*"He has looked on the humble estate of his servant. For behold,
from now on all generations will call me blessed."*
(Luke 1:48)

peaking of biblical songs, I love the Song of Solomon, a little book tucked rather obscurely into a handful of pages near the middle of the Bible. It tells the story of a king who, much to everyone's surprise, doesn't search for his bride among the sleek, beautiful women of the capital city.

Instead, he goes out into the countryside, into the rural areas, where he comes across a young woman toiling in her family's vineyard. Her skin is coarse and weathered, darkened by years of exposure to the workday sun. She smells of sweat and earth, not luxurious oils. Her beauty is raw and unpretentious, not polished.

How can it be that this is the woman a king would desire for his wife? She's absolutely amazed, astounded that he would ever give his heart to someone like her, someone bearing no pageantry or pedigree like the hundreds of others he could have selected from. You can sense her asking throughout the entire book, *Why would he have chosen me?* And yet no answer is given, except that he loves her. She, for his own reasons, is the one he wants.

Do you not hear some of this same emotion in the words of Mary's song? She, too, was just an ordinary young woman. Nothing indicates she'd been born into a wealthy, famous family. From all accounts, she was an average, small-town teenage girl, and likely no one within the slender orbit of her acquaintances envisioned a spectacular future ahead for her.

Yet watch what happened. *"God looked on the humble estate of his servant."* He shook this young girl's world one day, and everything changed. From that point forward, she said *"all generations will call me blessed."* And we, as members of one of those future generations more than two thousand years hence, can all attest to the accuracy of that statement. Her relationship with Jesus gave her life genuine significance.

This principle embedded in her statement is true not only of her but of us as well. When you think of yourself and your prospects for making much of a difference in the world, you may see only a plain, simple person without a lot of skills or promise or distinguishing characteristics. Nothing special. (On the other hand, you may feel that others should be more impressed than they seem to be with your training and gifts and contacts and potential.)

Only one thing matters, however, and it should serve as both an encourager and corrective to us. Having a relationship with the God of heaven makes *any* life extraordinary—and is *all* that makes a life extraordinary. Mary's experience of amazement can be yours as well when the Lord is with you and within you.

MY PRAYER

Father, what an awesome thought that You would choose me, though I have no merit of my own, nothing deserving of Your love and mercy. You have graciously accepted me through Christ and called me to reflect Your glory to others who need You as desperately as I do. Use my life for Your kingdom's purposes, and show Your greatness through my weakness, in Jesus' name.

———————◆———————

KEEP READING

— Deuteronomy 7:6–11
"It was not because you were more in number" (v. 7)

— Psalm 138:1–6
"For though the Lord is high, he regards the lowly" (v. 6)

— 1 Corinthians 1:26–29
"God chose what is low and despised in the world" (v. 28)

———————◆———————

MY RESPONSE

In your life, what are the Enemy's most potent, personal attacks against what God has said about you? How can you refute these lies daily, believing God will use your humble, available heart?

WHAT'S SO GREAT ABOUT IT?

*"He who is mighty has done great things for me,
and holy is his name."*
(Luke 1:49)

What if this Christmas season, you took every opportunity the Lord gives you to share a personal testimony with someone else about the "great things" He has done for you?

For many of us, that challenge may be outside of our comfort zone. It sounds like the "right thing" to do, but the whole idea can be a bit daunting. We fear making others (or ourselves) feel awkward or uneasy. Or perhaps, truth be told, you just feel as though any "great things" God may be doing in your life are outnumbered by all the other, not-so-great things you're enduring right now.

I'm glad that Christian faith does not require us to ignore or minimize our hurts, to act as if they don't exist, as if they shouldn't bother us. Pain, hardship, and heartache are unavoidable parts of our fallen world, even for believers. Our redemption, of course, has already been accomplished—through the cross and empty tomb—but our experience of it in real time is not complete. We don't yet know the unhindered joy we will one day feel when we are visibly in God's presence, away from all traces of the curse, with all things made new.

But if you're a child of God, no matter what may be going on in your life, you can lift your eyes upward from your circumstances. You can look beyond yourself and see that the God of the Bible is the God of today. He is the sovereign Lord over every moment of your life—past, present, and future. And He is always at work redeeming you. He is always actively engaged in giving you reason for rejoicing. Even if your eyes are legitimately, understandably filled with tears, He is still doing "great things" for you . . . "great things" worthy of your notice and worship, "great things" worthy of being told and talked about.

Mary probably had a million questions about why events were happening to her. How was she supposed to handle this pregnancy? How could she tell her parents? How did God expect her to get through this? Perhaps she laid out all these concerns to Elizabeth during the months she stayed at her house. But what we know for certain is that Mary embraced even her fears and apprehensions as an opportunity to exalt the Lord. And she not only felt the praise and gratitude in her own heart, but she expressed it verbally so that others could hear it and be blessed. She was overwhelmed that a holy God would notice her, that He would give her the privilege of playing a part in the Story of redemption, as that mission involved hardship on her part.

This song was her testimony. What's yours?

MY PRAYER

Lord, You do great things. Even in the midst of my most difficult seasons, You never stop performing supernatural acts in my life and on my behalf. Give me eyes of faith to see the "great things" You have done and are doing for me. And then help me share Your great works with others. May my thanks and worship include inviting others to witness what You alone can do, what You desire to do in all of us.

KEEP READING

— Job 5:8–16
"To God would I commit my cause, who does great things" (vv. 8–9)

— Psalm 126:1–6
"The Lord has done great things for us; we are glad" (v. 3)

— 1 John 4:13–16
"We know that we abide in him, and he in us" (v. 13)

MY RESPONSE

When's the last time you told someone about what God has done for you? How could you make this sharing a more frequent, habitual way of honoring Him for what He does?

THIS YEAR AND EVERY YEAR

*"His mercy is for those who fear him from
generation to generation."*
(Luke 1:50)

hristmas is sort of an annual marker. Arriving at the end of the year as it does, it causes us to look back and take stock, even as it causes us to look ahead and wonder. To hope. To imagine. Or perhaps, at times, to worry. To fear. But whatever you're feeling or dealing with as you draw deeper into the Christmas season this year, particularly if your joy is feeling muted by some loss or crisis or disappointment, I pray that this line in Mary's song will encourage your heart today.

It speaks to me of the unchanging character of God. The big theological word for it is *immutability*. God is "the same yesterday, today, and forever" (Heb. 13:8). Or as Mary put it, *"from generation to generation."*

This unchangeable aspect of His nature is something we need to be reminded of frequently. For even though Christmas can be highly predictable in its repeated traditions and interactions, it comes and finds us a year older now, perhaps in a different context, in a different stage of life. And, if we're not particularly pleased with our this-Christmas circumstances, it's easy to conclude that it's too late for God to change the ones that *could be* changed or to give us what we need for getting through the others.

Since I was a little girl, I have always loved reading books on the lives of great men and women of God from past generations. Although they, too, were saved sinners who experienced their good days and bad days, their overall example speaks to what God can do through anyone who puts his or her whole trust in Him.

The autobiography of George Mueller is one of those books that has left an impact on me. Mueller, you may know, established a number of orphanages in England during the 1800s, funding them entirely through prayer and faith and unwavering confidence in God's provision. Frequently in his journal, you'll find a passage that reads something like this: "We had nothing to eat. . . . We had no money to buy food. . . . We prayed and told God our needs. . . . God provided supernaturally." A day or two later, you'll find a similar account. And the next day or the next, again—the same thing. "We had nothing . . . we had no money . . . we prayed . . . God provided." Over and over again, Mueller recounted, God was unfailingly faithful in caring for thousands of orphans.

As you read this, behold your God. Behold Him more than a hundred years ago meeting the needs of His children who feared and trusted Him. Behold Him, because one of those children today is you. The times have changed, the names have changed, but God has not changed. As He has provided for past generations, so will He provide for you and me in this generation . . . and to every generation.

MY PRAYER

Heavenly Father, how I praise You today that You do not change. You are forever faithful. You will never be anything other than what You have always been—good, loving, powerful, pursuing, redeeming, restoring—changing us, but never changing Yourself. Such certainty emboldens me to pray today, knowing You will show Your strength and mercy as I keep looking to You in faith.

---◆---

KEEP READING

— Psalm 102:25–28
"You are the same, and your years have no end" (v. 27)

— Isaiah 51:12–16
"establishing the heavens and laying the foundations of the earth" (v. 16)

— 2 Timothy 2:8–13
"If we endure, we will also reign with him" (v. 12)

---◆---

MY RESPONSE

I hope you're continuing to let your heart and mind marinate day by day in these choice words of Scripture found in Mary's song. As you turn today's verse into prayer, what is He showing you?

WAIT AND SEE

"He has shown strength with his arm; he has scattered the proud in the thoughts of their hearts; he has brought down the mighty from their thrones and exalted those of humble estate."
(Luke 1:51–52)

God is sovereign. Everywhere in Scripture we're told of it. Though evil appears to triumph, the Lord has declared that He will have the final word.

In just a little while, the wicked will be no more;
 though you look carefully at his place, he will not be there.
But the meek shall inherit the land
 and delight themselves in abundant peace. (Ps. 37:10–11)

Mary knew these ways of God—His contempt for the proud, His heart for the humble, and His iron-clad assurance that His

Word will be accomplished, one way or another. In fact, she herself would have a front-row seat to witness one of history's greatest evidences that no one, no government, no opposition—nothing—can thwart the eternal plan of God.

The prophet Micah had said,

> *But you, O Bethlehem Ephrathah,*
>> *who are too little to be among the clans of Judah,*
> *from you shall come forth for me*
>> *one who is to be ruler in Israel,*
> *whose coming forth is from of old,*
>> *from ancient days.* (Micah 5:2)

Centuries ahead of time, God had spoken these words about His Son—the Messiah, His anointed One—who was now being carried in Mary's womb. Jesus was to be born in Bethlehem, the Bible said, in the southern part of Israel. But Mary didn't live in Bethlehem; she lived in Galilee, in the town of Nazareth, *north* of Israel.

Problem?

Not for a sovereign God. He simply acted through the tyrannical Caesar Augustus, founding emperor of the Roman Empire—who thought *he* was God—and led him to order an edict that would force Mary and Joseph to travel to Bethlehem at the time when she would be delivering her baby. "In those days a decree went out from Caesar Augustus that all the world should be registered"

(Luke 2:1). And Joseph, "because he was of the house and lineage of David" (v. 4), was required to register in Bethlehem.

That's the kind of God we serve! He is always orchestrating the events of this world, including the events in your own life, to accomplish His holy, eternal purposes, to see that His Word is fulfilled.

Whenever you feel as though your life or your situation is out of control, recall the contrast between a leader more powerful than any man in the first-century world and two nobodies who lived nowhere near the centers of cultural influence, completely subject to whatever orders this faraway ruler decided to give.

> *Wait for the LORD and keep his way,*
> > *and he will exalt you to inherit the land;*
> > *you will look on when the wicked are cut off.* (Ps. 37:34)

In the light of eternity, it will be just a little while before you see the proud scattered and the mighty brought down . . . before you see "those of humble estate" exalted.

MY PRAYER

Sovereign Lord, I bow before You today in humble submission and reverence for Your absolute sway over my life, indeed over the affairs of all the world. You who know the hearts of men, I ask that You act on behalf of those who are looking to You, trusting You. May I surrender fully to the authority of Your Word, knowing You are bringing your promises to complete fruition, in Jesus' name.

KEEP READING

— Psalm 27:7–14
"Be strong, and let your heart take courage" (v. 14)

— Luke 13:22–30
"Some are last who will be first, and some are first who will be last" (v. 30)

— 1 Peter 5:1–7
"Humble yourselves, therefore, under the mighty hand of God" (v. 6)

MY RESPONSE

In what areas of your life have you been resisting the call to humility, fearing it will make you lose ground that you've fought to capture? What would humility look like in this situation?

HUNGRY YET?

"He has filled the hungry with good things, and the rich
he has sent away empty."
(Luke 1:53)

What are you hungry for? Many of us associate Christmas with some favorite foods. Perhaps I could make you hungry right this moment, simply at the thought of looking forward to them. But Luke 1:53 brings another thought to mind: What are you *truly* hungry for? What do you *really* want in life more than anything? Depending on our answer to this question, we learn from God's Word what we can expect to receive.

Jesus said, "Blessed are those who hunger and thirst for righteousness, for they shall be satisfied" (Matt. 5:6). To the person who possesses an insatiable appetite and hunger for God, He will satisfy them with Himself, with His presence. From His "right hand" He will enable them to enjoy "pleasures forevermore" (Ps. 16:11). But in order to develop this type of hunger—which doesn't come naturally to any of us—we must daily remember and realize that we are "poor in spirit." We must recognize a need in ourselves that can only be filled by the God who promises "theirs is the kingdom of heaven" (Matt. 5:3).

Because look what happens to the "rich." They are "sent away empty." Mary wasn't referring here to the financially rich. There's nothing inherently wrong with being materially prosperous. But being self-righteous, self-sufficient—being full of oneself—is ultimately a recipe for spiritual starvation and stomachache.

Mary revealed her own heart's true hunger in how she responded to the angel Gabriel's message, after he'd told her what God had planned for her life. "Behold," she said, "I am the servant of the Lord; let it be to me according to your word" (Luke 1:38). To be God's "servant" (or as the King James Version says it, His "handmaid") represented in her time and place the lowest form of hired indenture. A handmaid had no plans of her own. She existed to serve her master. Her life was utterly at his disposal. Mary's reason for living, she was saying, was found in doing whatever would please the Lord.

No, the demands themselves may not have been in line with what she most wanted at the time. Not everything was immediately appetizing. But rather than being so full of herself that she felt entitled to resist Him, she believed the fulfillment He promised would prove far more satisfying than whatever she could obtain or protect by insisting on her way.

How many blessings do we miss experiencing because we try holding on to our lives, our reputations, our rights, our time, our convenience, our comfort? Those things are not what we most need. What we truly need are the "good things" He gives to all who are hungry. Hungry for only *one* thing. For Him.

MY PRAYER

Lord, You have allowed me to taste enough of the world's things to make me realize they have no lasting value. My need goes so much deeper. My need is for You. I ask You to keep this need ever before me, so You can make me an acceptable vessel for Your filling. And not for my filling alone, but so You can use my life to fill others with the bountiful blessings You alone provide.

KEEP READING

— Psalm 104:27–30
"When you open your hand, they are filled with good things" (v. 28)

— Mark 8:34–38
"For what does it profit a man to gain the whole world?" (v. 36)

— Ephesians 3:14–19
"Be filled with all the fullness of God" (v. 19)

MY RESPONSE

How full are you? If your most consistent answer is "Not very" or "Never enough to feel satisfied," try answering instead this better, more diagnostic question: How hungry are you?

WHEN MORNING BREAKS

"He has helped his servant Israel, in remembrance
of his mercy, as he spoke to our fathers, to Abraham
and to his offspring forever."
(Luke 1:54–55)

Do you remember the condition of Narnia when it first appears in C. S. Lewis' *The Lion, the Witch, and the Wardrobe*? It's always winter there, but never Christmas. The White Witch, who calls herself the queen of Narnia, has placed the land under a curse, leaving it covered in snow and ice, where it had remained for years and years.

The final book of the Old Testament ends with threats of a curse, with warnings of the judgment of God. "Behold, I will send you Elijah the prophet before the great and awesome day of the Lord comes. And he will turn the hearts of fathers to their children and the hearts of children to their fathers, lest I come and strike the land with a decree of utter destruction" (Mal. 4:5–6). If not for the covenant that God intended to reestablish, there would be no hope for the future. Either He would show us mercy, or else everything was over.

And that's where He left the world hanging for four hundred years, not saying another word to people on planet Earth. He understood, in order for the gospel to ever be good news to us, we would need to sit under the weight of not knowing. We would need to experience the heaviness of the curse—its darkness, its despair, its dismay.

Then finally, all those centuries later . . . a crack in the ice. An angel foretells the birth of John the Baptist (the "Elijah" in Malachi's prophecy). The forerunner of Messiah is coming. Though the news occurs quietly in a small corner of the world, it's like a little splash of joy, landing on frozen ground. Then an angel appears to Mary, a young girl in Nazareth. The Christ child, prophesied of old, is coming as a baby, born of a virgin. Another splash of joy, signaling the end of sin's rule and reign.

Generations of Old Testament believers, throughout those four hundred long years, had lived and died without ever seeing the fulfillment of the promises God had made in ages past. The easiest conclusion to draw was that He had abandoned His program, that His faithfulness was at an end.

But Mary knew different. She was there when the ice began to weaken and fracture. She was there when the blessing that God had decreed to Abraham came to life inside her teenage body. And having been there, she could know by faith (as we can) that the things spoken to Abraham long ago will continue unabated into the future, thawing the effects of the curse "to his offspring forever."

Mary's song ends where the fulfillment of God's promises began. We sing today because God remembered His covenant. We sing today because everything He has spoken, He will never fail to perform.

MY PRAYER

Lord, the evidence of Your kept promise is seen in the face of Jesus. You have lifted the curse. You have kept Your Word. I live with hope today because of Your faithfulness to Your people, redeeming and making all things new. During this season of Advent, remind me afresh that my future in You is equally sure, but only (again) in the face, in the name, of Jesus.

KEEP READING

— Genesis 12:1–3
"In you all the families of the earth shall be blessed" (v. 3)

— Psalm 89:29–37
"I will not violate my covenant or alter the word that went forth" (v. 34)

— Acts 3:19–26
"[God] sent him to you first, to bless you" (v. 26)

MY RESPONSE

Who in your life needs to be encouraged during this Christmas season that His promises are for sure, for now and forever? How can you help remind them of His trustworthiness?

ZECHARIAH'S SONG
"THE BENEDICTUS"

And his father Zechariah
was filled with the Holy Spirit
and prophesied, saying,

"Blessed be the Lord God of Israel,
for he has visited and redeemed his people
and has raised up a horn of salvation for us
in the house of his servant David,
as he spoke by the mouth of his holy prophets from of old,
that we should be saved from our enemies
and from the hand of all who hate us;

to show the mercy promised to our fathers
and to remember his holy covenant,
the oath that he swore to our father Abraham, to grant us
that we, being delivered from the hand of our enemies,
might serve him without fear,
in holiness and righteousness before him all our days.

And you, child, will be called the prophet of the Most High;
for you will go before the Lord to prepare his ways,
to give knowledge of salvation to his people
in the forgiveness of their sins,
because of the tender mercy of our God,
whereby the sunrise shall visit us from on high
to give light to those who sit in darkness and in the shadow of death,
to guide our feet into the way of peace."

(Luke 1:67–79)

CHRISTMAS VISIT

*"His father Zechariah was filled with the Holy Spirit
and prophesied, saying, "Blessed be the Lord God of Israel,
for he has visited and redeemed his people."*
(Luke 1:67–68)

echariah the priest, husband of Elizabeth, decided he'd heard enough from the neighbors and relatives, those who were trying to influence what these aging parents planned to name their now eight-day-old son. "His name is John," Zechariah emphatically wrote—not Junior!—his pen the only voice he'd been able to use since being reduced to silence nine months earlier.

Then the unexpected happened. Again.

"Immediately," the Bible says, God gave him back his speech (Luke 1:64). Finally, the gathered crowd could now hear what this awestruck father had been saving up to say. *Tell us more*, they were probably all thinking, *about why you insist on naming him John.*

And yet all he could talk about was—Jesus. The supreme miracle that Zechariah had been pondering throughout all those months of forced quiet was not the birth of his own son (amazing as that was) but that of the coming Messiah, the Christ—the soon-to-be living proof that God, after all these years, had "visited and redeemed his people."

Visitation. In a Christmas context, we think of visiting as a brief, lighthearted, and (hopefully) pleasant few days of company. But when God comes to visit, He means business. It's not a social call. According to Scripture, it means He's seen what's going on, He's concerned about His people's condition, and He's coming to do something about it, to deliver us from a problem we can't fix by ourselves.

Visitation is how the Bible described His actions toward ancient Israel after four hundred years of Egyptian bondage. Joseph had told them long beforehand, "God will visit you and bring you up out of this land to the land that he swore to Abraham, to Isaac, and to Jacob" (Gen. 50:24). Centuries later, upon the arrival of Moses, "when they heard that the LORD had visited the people of Israel and that he had seen their affliction, they bowed their heads and worshiped" (Exod. 4:31).

Zechariah did the same. In his song—the *Benedictus*—he recognized the day of divine visitation. As with Israel's deliverance from Egypt, Jesus' birth followed on the heels of another four-hundred-year interval of dark, lonely waiting. And as Zechariah's eyes were opened to see this new visitation approaching, he too opened his mouth in thanksgiving and worship.

Today we await one final visitation of Christ, now two thousand years in coming. (And counting.) But as the children of Israel could tell you, and as Zechariah could tell you, God often delays His visit past the point when people think it's actually going to happen. He's been a long time coming, yes, but "the Lord is not slow to fulfill his promise as some count slowness" (2 Pet. 3:9). He will visit again, as sure as He visited at Christmas.

And we can be worshiping Him for it now, in anticipation of the sure fulfillment of His promise.

MY PRAYER

Thank You, O Lord, for coming, for seeing, for knowing our plight, and for having mercy on our sinful, enslaved condition. Thank You, Immanuel—"God with us"—for not only visiting us but also staying with us by Your Holy Spirit. Keep us now as we await Your soon and sure return, Lord Jesus. We worship You today in confident faith and hope, with never-ending gratitude.

KEEP READING

— Psalm 106:1–12
"Remember me, O LORD, when you show favor to your people" (v. 4)

— Jeremiah 15:15–20
"Remember me and visit me" (v. 15)

— 2 Peter 3:8–13
"We are waiting for new heavens and a new earth in which righteousness dwells" (v. 13)

MY RESPONSE

Think of an example in your own life where you're waiting and praying for God's visitation. How different could this season of waiting be if you chose worship over impatience?

SEE THE LITTLE BABY

*". . . and has raised up a horn of salvation for us in the house
of his servant David, as he spoke by the mouth of
his holy prophets from of old."*
(Luke 1:69–70)

he little baby in the manger. That's the visual we see in our minds, the one we recreate in our homes when we set out the crèche each year, as I do in mine, with wispy pieces of straw all around. There's truth in that imagery, of course. It's how He came. As a tiny, newborn baby.

Just be sure, when you see the baby in the manger, you never forget who's actually lying there.

I recall being in Jackson Hole, Wyoming, one of my favorite vacation spots, riding with friends on an early morning drive to see some wildlife in its natural habitat. Off in a field, we saw a large herd of bison grazing. *Huge* animals—and yet so docile and nonthreatening looking. Their heads were lowered to the ground, seemingly disinterested in everything else around them. Signs in the area warned not to get within a hundred yards of these enormous beasts, even though from the look of them, you could almost picture yourself walking among them in the grass, happily running your fingers through their thick manes.

The signs, though, are there for a reason. Bison are highly protective of their young. They can accelerate up to thirty-five miles per hour, almost instantly. When people have ignored the posted advisories, wishing (like me) to snap a close-up picture, the bison have sometimes charged, goring them with their horns, flinging them like rag dolls into the air.

The horns on a bison are a symbol of power, of strength. Far from being merely a design element, they are a deadly weapon. In Old Testament times the horns of wild animals were often used in battle, wielded by a warrior attacking his enemies.

So when Zechariah prophesied about the "horn of salvation" that God had "raised up," he was declaring what this little baby in the manger was coming into the world to do—to deal with and defeat our archenemy. As David had said years earlier, "The LORD is my rock and my fortress and my deliverer, my God, my rock, in whom I take refuge, my shield, and the horn of my salvation, my stronghold and my refuge, my savior" (2 Sam. 22:2–3).

Jesus, the child that Zechariah knew would be born, is a powerful Savior and King—which is just the kind we need— because sin is powerful, and Satan is powerful. But "blessed be the

Lord God of Israel, for he has visited and redeemed his people and has raised up a horn of salvation for us," against whom Satan and all his minions are no match, and through whom all the corruption of our hearts can be utterly conquered. No one and nothing in this whole world can defeat Him—this tiny baby in the manger.

MY PRAYER

Lord, You are marvelous in power. You are mighty to save. I magnify Your name in my heart today, longing to see You as You really are—stronger than all my sin and temptation, greater than every struggle that opposes me. I know my trust in You is well-placed because You alone are able to do all You have promised . . . because You alone are my salvation.

KEEP READING

— Exodus 15:6–12
"Your right hand, O LORD, glorious in power" (v. 6)

— Psalm 66:1–7
"awesome in his deeds toward the children of men" (v. 5)

— Hebrews 2:14–18
"[that] he might destroy the one who has the power of death" (v. 14)

MY RESPONSE

Why would your Enemy want to diminish your view of God's limitless power? What has he tried to convince you is more powerful than your Savior's ability to conquer and overcome?

HIGHER DEFINITION

*". . . that we should be saved from our enemies and from
the hand of all who hate us."*
(Luke 1:71)

he Bible contains certain words that, although not entirely
unique to our Christian faith, come alive with immeasurably
more meaning when touched by the biblical message of Christmas.

One of these words is *salvation*.

Everyone, of course, understands to some degree the concept
of being saved. We've seen people saved from rising floodwaters
after a major storm. We've known of firefighters and other first
responders who've saved lives during an emergency. Being saved
is to be rescued; being saved is to be delivered from distress and
danger. The whole concept of salvation implies being saved *from*
something, whether saved out of financial ruin or saved on an

operating table. It means being saved from an enemy that threatens to destroy us.

Or as Zechariah said it: "*saved from our enemies and from the hand of all who hate us.*"

A first-century Jew, hearing of this salvation Zechariah was describing, would have equated "enemies" with the domineering presence of their Roman occupiers, just as anyone today could quickly name the present troubles they most wish to be delivered from. But Zechariah, under the inspiration of the Holy Spirit, was speaking of far greater enemies than mere political oppression. He was speaking of salvation from the ultimate enemies of sin, death, and Satan, as well as from the righteous wrath of God's judgment on all unrighteous humanity. Who could *ever* save us from powers such as these? What amount of human resistance is sufficient to overcome them?

That's why Zechariah's song is a Christmas song . . . because this is why Jesus was coming, "to seek and save the lost" (Luke 19:10). "You shall call his name Jesus," the angel said to Joseph, "for he will save his people from their sins" (Matt. 1:21). The name Jesus (such a precious name) is the Greek form of the Hebrew *Yeshuah*, which means "Jehovah is salvation." And the word salvation (such a precious word) derives its highest meaning from the rescue mission that Jesus came to perform for us, saving us from the spiritual forces that held our hearts and souls captive.

But even those who know salvation primarily by its common, earthly definition understand something we should apply to our hearts as well. Once a person has been delivered from a dire circumstance, the last place they willingly want to place themselves is back under its power. They don't run back into bankruptcy, for example, any more than they'd run back into a burning building. If we would truly recognize the life-threatening danger that sin posed (and still poses) to us—the great enemy from which Jesus came to save us—we would want nothing at all to do with it.

The closer we come to knowing what salvation really means, the further away we'll stay from the sin that made us need saving in the first place.

MY PRAYER

Lord, too rarely do I stop to think how great is my need for salvation, the depths of sin I've needed saving from. But throughout this Christmas season—and every day—I want to savor the wonder of Your salvation. I praise You, Father, for sending Your Son on an errand of such grace and power. Through faith in Him, I am saved from my enemies today. Help me declare it with my life and my lips.

KEEP READING

— Psalm 40:9–10
"I have told the glad news of deliverance in the great congregation" (v. 9)

— Isaiah 33:1–6
"He will be the stability of your times, abundance of salvation" (v. 6)

— 1 Thessalonians 5:5–11
"For God has not destined us for wrath, but to obtain salvation" (v. 9)

MY RESPONSE

Even if you've known Christ for many years, how have you experienced His salvation from sin in recent days? How is the gospel continuing to deliver you?

FAMILY LINE

". . . to show the mercy promised to our fathers and
to remember his holy covenant, the oath that he swore
to our father Abraham."
(Luke 1:72–73)

here were no stockings hung on the mantelpiece in the home of Zechariah and Elizabeth. But if this family ever did find occasion for posting their names all together in a row, in such a visual fashion, the meanings behind their monikers could have lined up to fill a whole room with Christmas promise.

Zechariah. His name means "God remembers." The deliverance and salvation that Zechariah celebrated in his hymn went back many centuries, nearly all the way to the beginning of time. When the first man and first woman fell into sin, the Lord prophetically told the serpent how the offspring of Adam and Eve's union (an early biblical picture of Christ) would "bruise your head," even though Satan would "bruise his heel" (Gen. 3:15).

From that point forward, in an unbroken line throughout the remainder of the Old Testament, one after another of God's prophets spoke of the coming Savior, the Redeemer. Seasons came along when it *seemed* as if God had forgotten, but "not one word has failed of all his good promise" (1 Kings 8:56). God remembers.

Elizabeth. Her name means "the oath of God," a word that Zechariah paired with the "holy covenant" which God had remembered—"the oath that he swore to our father Abraham." Out of the seed of Abraham, whom God chose to be the fountainhead of the covenant, the Lord would bless not only His own chosen people but all the nations of the earth. The "oath" of God—it means something; it stands for something; it tells of a covenant-making and covenant-keeping God.

And then *John.* He was barely a week old at the time, but his name captures well the theme that Zechariah's entire song commemorates: "the grace of God." God's grace is the reason why all the undergirding faithfulness that flows beneath His oath and covenant is able to blossom into our lives. Apart from His divine intervention, not only are we dead in our sins, and not only do we have no hope of eternal life . . . we don't even know enough to cry out to Him for help. In our natural state, we are so broken, so undone, that God had to initiate even our desire for Him. But because of His grace—the unearned, undeserved favor of God— He invites us to partake in these promises. All of grace, none of works. All of Christ, none of ourselves.

How beautiful that God, in His supernatural wisdom and providence, brought together in one family such a linear formation of heavenly truth.

"God remembers"—"the oath of God"—"the grace of God"

May our own families communicate an equally clear gospel message of the liberty and hope He offers . . . from the decorations on the wall to the spiritual DNA in our homes and hearts.

MY PRAYER

Thank You, Father, not only for embedding Your image into our identities, but for writing our names on the palms of Your hands. Thank You for designing us to show forth the greatness of our Creator, and for choosing through Your Son to become our Redeemer. We depend each day on Your promises—on Your oath and Your covenant in Christ—and ever on Your grace.

KEEP READING

— Psalm 105:7–11
"He remembers his covenant forever" (v. 8)

— Isaiah 43:1–3a
"I have called you by name, you are mine" (v. 1)

— Hebrews 3:1–6
"And we are his house if indeed we hold fast our confidence" (v. 6)

MY RESPONSE

Try discovering the meaning of your own name and those of others in your family. How could you perhaps do something tangible that symbolizes these meanings, tying them to God's purpose in your lives?

SERVICE CALL

*". . . that we, being delivered from the hand of our enemies,
might serve him without fear, in holiness and
righteousness before him all our days."*
(Luke 1:74–75)

By far, more than any other time of year, Christmas inspires a noble increase in acts of service and generosity, not only among Christians but throughout the entire population. The church, in fact (I'd say), is often outdone by unbelievers in showing sacrificial kindness to others.

This wouldn't be the case, however, if we took to heart, as well as to mind, the lessons to be learned from these final thoughts in Zechariah's first (long) sentence. Here are three:

1. *We are saved to serve.* The themes of salvation that run so profusely throughout this Christmas song describe much more than the transaction of becoming born again. God saves us for

a purpose. He saves us to serve Him. Why would He deliver us from what our self-centered ways have done to us, only to turn us loose to keep following our own paths? We obviously were being destroyed by the yoke of sin and Satan, and God in His grace removed it from around our shame-heavy shoulders. But the place where we find "rest for [our] souls" (Matt. 11:29) is inside the yoke of Christ.

Having been "delivered from the hand of our enemies," our path into freedom is found in serving Him with gratitude, serving Him with gladness. We are not saved as an end in itself but as an entryway into service.

2. *Service is worship; worship is service.* We tend to categorize these practices into two separate subsets of Christian living. Service, we think, is for a particular day and clothing, while worship belongs to another day and a somewhat dressier ensemble. But Zechariah's word choice for how we should "serve him" is biblically interchangeable with how we should worship him. The two words are so closely aligned as to be nearly synonymous— service naturally flowing from worship; worship naturally flowing from service. We worship God by serving Him; we exist to serve Him worshipfully.

3. *There is no fear in love.* Few things in life are more cheerless and ineffective than trying to placate God with acts of service and worship. Truly He is a God of immense, indescribable power— fearsome indeed in the face of human sin. But His salvation means we now stand "holy and blameless" in His presence (Eph. 1:4). The fear motivation has been lifted. *We're free*—free to "serve him

81

without fear, in holiness and righteousness before him all our days." Not because we must (or else!), but because we've been redeemed from our "dead works to serve the living God" (Heb. 9:14).

The same gospel that changed the condition of our hearts is intended also to change the movements of our hands and feet. Feel free to serve and worship, having been freed to worship and serve.

MY PRAYER

O Father, if Your only Son was willing to empty Himself, coming here to be offered as a selfless sacrifice, surely I am called to lay down my life as well. Give me a servant's heart. Open my eyes to others' needs, and help me give freely, without fear, in Your name. Expand my vision of what You've saved me to do: to worship You, to serve You.

KEEP READING

— Psalm 100:1–5
"Serve the LORD with gladness" (v. 2)

— Micah 6:6–8
"He has told you, O man, what is good" (v. 8)

— 1 John 4:16–21
"We love because he first loved us" (v. 19)

MY RESPONSE

What are some of the practical implications of seeing worship and service as a synonymous experience? What kind of impact could it produce on the rest of your Christmas season?

TRAIN UP A CHILD

"And you, child, will be called the prophet of the Most High; for you will go before the Lord to prepare his ways."
(Luke 1:76)

When you think of John the Baptist, perhaps your mental image goes quickly to locusts and wild honey, or perhaps to some other element of his bold ministry style. But what I find particularly riveting is a statement John made to his disciples, once Jesus started to draw the large crowds that used to flock to hear him. *Don't worry*, he essentially said to them, *this is the way it's supposed to be.* "He must increase, but I must decrease" (John 3:30).

The only thing that mattered to him was that Jesus be magnified. What a grand, noble way to live one's life.

But I don't believe he just came up with that line out of thin air one day when the moment called for it. I think the reason he could give such a profound, quotable answer—rich in genuine humility and exaltation of Christ—is because it's what he'd been taught as a child, from as far back as he could remember. His parents, Zechariah and Elizabeth, instilled in him a sense of God's mission and purpose for his life from the cradle up. John had always known he'd be a "prophet of the Most High; for you will go before the Lord to prepare his ways."

This is why you were born, my son.

I love that. And I'd suggest to you today that this declaration of identity and calling is something that not only the parents of a John the Baptist should do. Every child needs to be told that God put him or her on this earth for a reason, with a role to play, and with a calling to a God-honoring way of living.

I realize, if you're a parent or grandparent, if you're an aunt or uncle, the children in your life were not specifically prophesied in Isaiah 40, as John was. No angel appeared announcing their birth, saying, "He will go before him in the spirit of Elijah" (Luke 1:17). But still, you can lead your children to the Word. You can show them God's promises. You can help them understand they weren't born to serve themselves or seek to be entertained. Just as John prepared the way for Christ to come physically the first time, they and all of us are here to prepare the way for Him to come to others' hearts and lives.

Give them a biblical vision for their lives.

Your children, if you're blessed to have them, are each gifted and talented. They will go on and continue to do many different things in life. But no matter what kind of work they'll do in the marketplace or the arts or in their communities or as a parent, they are here on mission, on purpose. God has placed them here to know Him, enjoy Him, and make Him known.

And they need to know that.

MY PRAYER

Lord, You have implanted within us a mission and purpose, not only for the entirety of our lives but one that colors how we should conduct ourselves today, this week, and at special times like these. Help us be faithful to Your Word, true to Your calling, and trusting in Your promises. And help us teach our children well, that they may absorb and capture this same vision for themselves.

———————◆———————

KEEP READING

— Deuteronomy 4:5–9
"Make them known to your children" (v. 9)

— Psalm 139:13–16
"For I am fearfully and wonderfully made" (v. 14)

— 2 Timothy 1:5–14
"Fan into flame the gift of God, which is in you" (v. 6)

———————◆———————

MY RESPONSE

What are some of the daily opportunities God gives you to "prepare his ways" into the hearts of others? How could you help your children be mindful and watchful for these in their own lives?

O, THE DEEP, DEEP LOVE

". . . to give knowledge of salvation to his people in the forgiveness of their sins, because of the tender mercy of God."
(Luke 1:77–78)

You may or may not have a hard time believing this. But God doesn't just love you. He feels His *love* for you. And because He *feels* such love for you, He *acts* on the basis of His love for you. He *moves* toward you. He *does* things for you.

You have no idea how much God loves you.

But I'm about to give you a word for it. When Zechariah spoke of the "tender mercy" God shows toward sinners—toward me, toward you—the "tender" part of that phrase is the Greek word *splanchnon* (SPLANK-non). It's unfamiliar sounding, I know, but you'll start to glean a better sense of it when I tell you it's where we get our English word *spleen*. It's a deeply felt mercy, one that comes from way, way down inside. It's what the older Bible translations call the "bowels of compassion" (1 John 3:17 kjv). It's internal. It hurts.

But *splanchnon* doesn't just ache, it acts.

It doesn't stop at merely feeling bad. It moves. It does something.

The word actually shows up all throughout the Gospels in the heart and ministry of Jesus. Do you remember the widow weeping over the casket of her dead son? "When the Lord saw her, his heart went out to her" (Luke 7:13 niv)—*splanchnon*—and He raised the young man from the dead.

When Jesus saw the crowds waiting for Him on the seashore, "he had compassion on them"—*splanchnon*—"and healed their sick" (Matt. 14:14). When He saw them hungry He felt, again—*splanchnon*—and fed them by the thousands with a handful of fish and loaves (Matt. 15:32).

Blind men along the road outside of Jericho (Matt. 20:34). Lepers falling on their knees before Him in Galilee (Mark 1:41). The Good Samaritan coming across the man beaten senseless by robbers (Luke 10:33). The father of the Prodigal Son catching sight of him in the distance (Luke 15:20). *Splanchnon*.

It's how God feels and acts toward us, who were hopelessly trapped in our sins. It's what Jesus lived out on the earth, delivering healing and wholeness to those He touched. And as people who've been loved by God, who've become wholly unworthy recipients of His heart-rending mercy, we are called now to demonstrate these same tender mercies to others. "Put on then, as God's chosen ones, holy and beloved, compassionate hearts" (Col. 3:12). *Splanchnon*. Don't just wish others weren't hurting and in need. Do something. Say something. Go to them. Have mercy on them.

The Lord knew our sins could never be forgiven if they must always be measured against His justice. So He extended His mercy—deep, gut-level, *splanchnon* mercy—so we could experience salvation and be set free from the punishment our guilt had cost us.

That's God and His love for you. Do you see how much He loves you?

MY PRAYER

Lord, why should You care about me in my sins? Why would you do anything kind toward someone like me, who made myself an enemy of Yours, and often still demands my own way in the face of Your all-wise, all-loving will? Praise You, my Lord, for Your tender mercy. Praise You for looking on me with love. Praise You today, in the tender, compassionate name of Jesus.

KEEP READING

— Psalm 103:8–14
"The LORD is merciful and gracious" (v. 8)

— Isaiah 49:13–15
"Can a woman forget her nursing child?" (v. 15)

— Titus 3:3–7
"He saved us . . . according to his own mercy" (v. 5)

MY RESPONSE

Where or with whom might God be especially convicting you this Christmas to demonstrate a deeper heart of compassion? Perhaps you could write out your desire for it as a specific prayer.

NIGHT AND DAY

". . . whereby the sunrise shall visit us from on high to give light to those who sit in darkness and in the shadow of death, to guide our feet into the way of peace."
(Luke 1:78–79)

echariah's song ends with a beginning. With a sunrise. The day of Christ's appearing was drawing near.

Isn't that what we're feeling now? Isn't it what we feel every year when the days are winding down toward Christmas, when the excitement is building up for those things we most enjoy about this glorious moment on the calendar?

I confess, I don't see a lot of sunrises in person. Most days, the sun has already begun its usual ascent into the sky by the time I begin my morning. But I took a field trip not long ago, rousing from bed before daybreak, to see what I've been missing. And I was reminded again of what Zechariah saw in his mind's eye when he looked ahead to the birth of the Messiah.

He obviously saw first the darkness. Sunrise would be unnecessary if the world was continually in light. Zechariah knew and saw and spoke of the darkness then, just as we know and see and speak of the darkness now. Imagine, though, "the distress and darkness, the gloom of anguish" (Isa. 8:22) that draped itself upon the world before Jesus ever came and stepped into it.

But the darkness was breaking. Zechariah could tell. It wouldn't immediately disappear, like when a light is suddenly ignited in a darkened room, jolting everyone awake all at once. As with the sunrise that still happens each morning, the darkness dissipates gradually. In fact, it's hard to identify the exact moment when you'd call it "light." It's a slow, gentle, subtle, almost imperceptible transition between gray hues and brightness.

Jesus' coming was the same way. His was a quiet, humble birth, occurring in relative obscurity. Few in that day recognized what was happening. And even these hundreds of years later, many people still don't realize that the sun has risen upon us, that the dawn has come. They remain locked in the "shadow of death," unaware that Christ has come to bring them—them *personally*—into the light.

But light was coming, and now has come, and has appeared "from on high." No government official or department is in charge of throwing the switch for the sunrise. Though our lives depend on what each morning's sunrise produces, we can do nothing to cause or hurry it. God sovereignly determined the moment when He would literally, physically send Christ to light our darkness. And he chose Zechariah and his son John as heralds to shatter the long prophetic silence.

Sunrise was coming.

The promise of the sunrise is what makes the darkness bearable, including the gray days of waiting which Zechariah knew too well. Join Him today in looking to the heavens, "because your redemption is drawing near" (Luke 21:28).

MY PRAYER

Father God, thank You for bringing the sunrise. Thank You for not leaving us in darkness, in the shadow of death, but for brightening our lives with Your saving presence. We know You've sent Your Son now, and we know He is coming again. But help us watch for Him today, from morning till night—following Him, serving Him, walking in His light in everything we do.

KEEP READING

— Genesis 1:1–5
"And God said, 'Let there be light'" (v. 3)

— Psalm 119:145–148
"I rise before dawn and cry for help" (v. 147)

— John 1:1–13
"In him was life, and the life was the light of men" (v. 4)

MY RESPONSE

Having worked slowly through this song of Zechariah, try taking time today to reread his *Benedictus* from beginning to end. What stands out to you now that you'd not seen before?

THE ANGELS' SONG
"GLORIA!"

And the angel said to them,

"Fear not, for behold,
I bring you good news of great joy
that will be for all the people.
For unto you is born this day in the city of David
a Savior, who is Christ the Lord.
And this will be a sign for you:
you will find a baby
wrapped in swaddling cloths
and lying in a manger."

And suddenly there was with the angel
a multitude of the heavenly host
praising God and saying,

"Glory to God in the highest,
and on earth peace
among those with whom he is pleased!"

(Luke 2:10–14)

WHATEVER YOU SAY

In the same region there were shepherds out in the field, keeping watch over their flock by night. And an angel of the Lord appeared to them, and the glory of the Lord shone around them, and they were filled with great fear.
(Luke 2:8–9)

With approximately three hundred references to them in Scripture, you'd think we'd be "well versed" in our knowledge of angels: who they are, what they do, how they operate. Instead most of what's considered common knowledge about angels is largely untrue, when evaluated in the light of Scripture. But since their appearances are such a frequent part of the Christmas narrative, we can discover a lot of fresh detail to the old familiar story by understanding what all these angels were doing there.

David said in Psalm 103, "Praise the LORD, you his angels, you mighty ones who do his bidding, who obey his word. Praise the

LORD, all his heavenly hosts, you his servants who do his will" (vv. 20–21 NIV). Therefore we know these angels are "mighty" creatures, which explains why even one angel's presence could fill a rough-hewn, gritty group of shepherds with fear.

We know they're "heavenly" beings, which explains why their visible appearance on earth would emanate "the glory of the Lord," the manifest presence of God. But more than anything, we know they do God's "bidding," they obey His "word," they follow His "will." They are God's servants who carry out His business in the world, and their primary job—their one, eternal calling—is to serve Him and bring Him pleasure.

So they came where they were told on this night when Jesus was born in Bethlehem—first one angel, to be followed by others. For they had known the Son of God since they were first created. They knew His intimate relationship with the Father. They knew the love and oneness that the Trinity shared. And yet, Jesus had chosen to leave behind what He'd experienced for all eternity— the fellowship, the communion, the joy, the intimacy—to come down to this messed-up, prodigal planet. Why?

Here's why: "I delight to do your will, O my God" (Ps. 40:7–8). Jesus said, "My food is to do the will of him who sent me and to accomplish his work" (John 4:34). These heavenly angels knew the Son had been sent here, and He had come at His Father's pleasure. So when they were sent, they did the same thing. Giving God pleasure is what angels do.

But actually, it's what all of us are called to do, and should *delight* to do—the doing of His will; obedient to His bidding—

"for thou hast created all things, and for thy pleasure they are and were created" (Rev. 4:11 KJV). When you hear the angels' song, don't hear only the rhythmic words you've known since you were a child. See them doing the Father's pleasure, as Jesus was doing the Father's pleasure, as you and I are to live to do the Father's pleasure.

MY PRAYER

I am Yours, Lord, to do whatever You please. I am Yours, Lord, to send wherever You desire to send me. Sanctify my heart until the only thing that moves me is being moved at the pleasure of Your will. Thank You for the angelic reminder that my business is to be about my Father's business. "Your kingdom come, your will be done, on earth as it is in heaven" (Matt. 6:10).

KEEP READING

— Joshua 24:14–18
"Therefore we also will serve the LORD" (v. 18)

— Psalm 147:7–11
"The LORD takes pleasure in those who fear him" (v. 11)

— Hebrews 13:20–21
"working in us that which is pleasing in his sight" (v. 21)

MY RESPONSE

To what pleasures do you find yourself clinging, other than what pleases God? What would change if you began thinking in terms of always doing the Lord's pleasure?

GOOD FOR ALL AGES

And the angel said to them, "Fear not, for behold, I bring you good news of great joy that will be for all the people."
(Luke 2:10)

The Roman establishment had a version of what it considered "good news." Whenever its officials proclaimed the great deeds of Emperor Augustus, adopted son of Julius Caesar, they used a Greek term as part of the inscription: *euangelion* (yoo-ang-GHEL-ee-on), which is translated *gospel* or *good news*.

But when God proclaimed "good news" by angelic messenger to a band of shepherds up the road a piece from Bethlehem, it was news that mattered to "all the people," not only those who belonged to a certain class or political persuasion. Compared to what filtered down to the masses from the Roman propaganda mill, the news of Jesus' birth was a gospel entirely different—a difference maker for people who hadn't heard any *real* "good news" in a really long time.

Like these shepherds, for instance. Shepherding was low on the totem pole of desirable vocations. These men gutted out their hard labors each day with little payback to cheer them or to provide much hope for the future. Shepherds were anonymous. Their names don't even appear in the Bible's inspired telling of the Christmas account. They had no power or influence—poor and uneducated, unskilled for most other kinds of work that might have earned them a chance to climb from the bottom rungs of the social ladder.

And that wasn't all. When people would go to offer their sacrifices, in observance of God's instructions for obtaining forgiveness for sins, shepherds weren't usually able to attend. They were always keeping an eye on the sheep. And because they couldn't often celebrate these Sabbaths, they were regarded as outcasts in Israel, ceremonially unclean.

The only thing for which they were truly qualified was needing some good news.

But the truth is, *all* people can fit that job description. Maybe one of those people at this particular holiday time is you. I realize as we approach the last few sunrises before Christmas morning, that not every home is bursting with joy and excitement. As exhilarating as Christmas can feel when in the midst of enjoying certain life stages, it can also land with a seasonally enhanced thud of pain, grief, and loneliness when you find yourself dealing with hard things.

But the birth of Jesus Christ is not good news just for *some* people. Nor is it good news only for those in pleasant, congenial circumstances. The song of the angel is good news that eclipses and overshadows whatever else is happening in your life right now. It's what "all the people" need, for *all* the things that threaten to deprive us of joy.

Any other kind of good news is only temporary, subject to being upended by bad news, and always open to someone else's interpretation. But this Christmas, stand amazed with the shepherds at news that's good for everyone, able to counter even the worst case of disappointment or despair.

MY PRAYER

Lord, thank You for reminding me just how good Your good news really is. You are no respecter of persons. You delight in revealing Yourself to those who are the most unlikely of earthly favor. And You care for all of us in our hurts and sadness and suffering. May I spend these special days with my eyes on You, on the Christ child, and on my gratitude for Your generous blessing.

KEEP READING

— Psalm 90:14–17
"Let the favor of the Lord our God be upon us" (v. 17)

— Isaiah 61:1–3
"to bring good news to the poor" (v. 1)

— Titus 2:11–14
"bringing salvation for all people." (v. 11)

MY RESPONSE

Count up as many examples of blessing as you can name from the good news of Jesus' coming into the world. Keep adding to it through the week, finding your joy in His gospel this Christmas.

EXPECTING THE UNSUSPECTED

*"For unto you is born this day in the city of David a Savior,
who is Christ the Lord. And this will be a sign for you:
you will find a baby wrapped in swaddling cloths
and lying in a manger."*
(Luke 2:11–12)

I f you're a watcher of Britain's royal family, you likely keep close tabs on those rare occasions when a new heir or heiress is expected to be born. Reporters and photographers camp outside the hospital, eager for updates, wanting to be first to capture the images and story lines. According to tradition, once the child arrives, an official birth announcement is rushed by courier to be displayed outside Buckingham Palace for public viewing. During one of the more recent arrivals of a newborn prince, ardent followers were typing and sending an estimated 25,000 tweets per *minute* sharing their first thoughts and opinions. Five percent of all global news being reported that day revolved around the birth of the royal baby.

What a contrast to how God chose to handle the birth of the Lord Jesus.

Doesn't it strike you as fascinating that His plan to reveal such earth-shaking news was so different from the way we do our public relations today? If such a baby had been born in our times, there'd be the buildup, the news coverage, the magazine covers in the grocery aisles. And it wouldn't be relegated to a small, insignificant, hard-to-reach village, but rather to the modern-day equivalent of a London or Los Angeles or some other media-centric city of the world.

Instead, not even Caesar knew this moment was happening. Herod, the man delegated to maintain governance over this region of the Roman empire, had no clue what was going on. Neither did the Jewish religious leaders, who at least possessed evidence from biblical prophecy, pointing however mysteriously to just such an event. During those hours when Jesus Christ, the Son of God, was being "born in the likeness of men" (Phil. 2:7), the only people on the planet made aware of it were a handful of simple, humble shepherds working the graveyard shift in rural pastureland.

And as to the clothes that Jesus was brought home in or the outfitting of His nursery, the pictures wouldn't be making the rounds of celebrity websites, nor emulated by other young moms who were expecting their own babies in the ensuing months. The angels were not embarrassed to report that the child—fully human yet fully divine—could be found nearby "wrapped in swaddling cloths and lying in a manger."

How different. How wondrously different.

How clear that God's ways are beautifully not our ways.

"Unto you is born this day in the city of David a Savior *[come to save us from our sins]*, who is Christ *[the anointed one, the promised Messiah]* the Lord *[God in flesh]*."

This was not just another baby, not even another royal baby to be heralded by appropriate privilege and protocol. God had His own way of making the announcement.

God has His own ways.

MY PRAYER

You amaze me, Lord. How can One of such indescribable power restrain Himself to simplicity and secrecy? O how You put to shame our proud human plans and our love for ourselves! Instead You show us another way—the way of humility and purity, the way of quietness and contentment. I rest today in Your hands, You whose ways are far greater than my ways.

KEEP READING

— Psalm 119:14–16
"In the way of your testimonies I delight" (v. 14)

— Isaiah 55:6–11
"For my thoughts are not your thoughts" (v. 8)

— Romans 11:33–36
"How inscrutable his ways" (v. 33)

MY RESPONSE

How can your recognition of His ways influence some of the worldly patterns you've adopted into your own life? What are one or two practical applications you can draw from His methods?

PRAISE SONG

And suddenly there was with the angel a multitude of the heavenly host praising God and saying, "Glory to God in the highest, and on earth peace among those with whom he is pleased."
(Luke 2:13–14)

Angels do a lot of things. They minister strength and sustenance to believers here on earth. They protect the people of God. They assist us in spiritual warfare against the forces of Satan and evil. They rejoice at our repentance. One day, they'll even join with Jesus in the execution of His final judgment. They have many jobs and assignments to do.

But, my, do they know how to praise!

Praising God is what angels do.

It's certainly what they did on this night, more than two thousand years ago. No Christmas program or worship service has ever rivaled it, before or since. None of the shepherds in attendance on that Judean hillside was stifling a yawn or wishing this whole thing would hurry up and be over. I believe they were enthralled, mesmerized. In fact, they likely got caught up in the moment and began participating in the praise themselves. I think their hearts were drawn into it, the way people of faith always resonate with authentic worship.

Now we don't know if the angels—plural at this point, apparently *many* plural—actually sang the words that appear in our Bible. As with Elizabeth's and Mary's and Zechariah's songs before, we only know they've been delivered to us in print as hymns or poems of the first Christmas.

But it was praise at a whole other level. And though it lasted for only a single verse in Scripture before "the angels went away from them into heaven" (v. 15), I feel sure they returned only to keep praising God around His throne, just as they were doing before He'd sent them to earth to share a taste of it with the shepherds.

But think of it. Think of who angels are, and why they'd feel so motivated to praise. They themselves are not sinful creatures. They have no need of redemption, as we do. And yet, they were ecstatic seeing this plan to redeem fallen sinners begin to take shape in time and space. They'd been waiting for eons to see God reveal it. And since we know there is "joy in heaven over one sinner who repents" (Luke 15:7), their joy went through the roof at witnessing the precise hour when the Savior of the world was sent down to bring "peace" to those—*all* of those—who would place their faith in Him, in Jesus.

So today, tonight, as you do what you do to celebrate Christmas Eve, I urge you—as one like all the rest of us sinful human beings who depend on this Christ child as our hope for salvation and forgiveness—outdo the angels in expressing your praise. Rejoice at what Jesus came to this earth to accomplish.

And may you go to bed tonight not wanting the worship to end at your house, but to spread throughout the world.

MY PRAYER

Praise You, Lord—for seeing our need for a Savior. Praise You, Lord—for imagining a solution no one else would ever have thought possible. Praise You, Lord—for loaning Your angels to us in that moment to help us see just how special Your gift truly is. And praise You, Lord—for an eternity to spend in celebration of what You have done. Praise, O praise You, Lord!

KEEP READING

— 1 Chronicles 16:23–27
"Great is the LORD, and greatly to be praised" (v. 25)

— Psalm 150:1–6
"Let everything that has breath praise the LORD" (v. 6)

— Revelation 19:6–10
"For the Lord our God the Almighty reigns" (v. 6)

MY RESPONSE

Praise Him!

THIS CHANGES EVERYTHING

*And the shepherds returned, glorifying and praising God for all
who had heard and seen, as it had been told them.*
(Luke 2:20)

he shepherds were never the same. Christmas should do that
to us. Being here celebrating it again, being face to face with
what it means ... we should never be the same after that. Christmas
changes things.

Perhaps, as some of us can tend to think, you hear someone
speak about being different because of what Christ has done for
us, and you take it as a challenge. You, too, believe you should be
different because of it, so you add it to your list. You're going to
work at this. You're going to do like the lady said.

But here's what I find so sweet about what God did for the
shepherds. He put faith in their hearts to continue believing

what they'd just seen. This was *God's* work, everything that had happened leading up to the angels' song. And it would be His work to keep changing the shepherds' hearts after the angels had gone away and they couldn't hear them anymore, just as it is His work to keep changing *us* after we've opened all the gifts and put the decorations away.

So let's see what we should expect Him to do, by seeing what He did for the shepherds "which the Lord has made known to us" (Luke 2:15).

"And they went with haste and found Mary and Joseph, and the baby lying in the manger. And when they saw it, they made known the saying that had been told them concerning this child" (vv. 16–17). They couldn't keep it to themselves. God chose these lowly, unknown shepherds not only to be the first to *hear* this wonderful news but also the first to *share* it with others. As we seek Him and ask Him to change us, He will give us opportunities to tell of this baby, this Savior, born for our salvation.

"And all who heard it wondered at what the shepherds told them" (v. 18). It is not our job to convince people about the truth of what God has done for us (and for them) through Christ. Our job is only to keep celebrating and sharing the Good News of His coming and His redemption, and He will cause others to marvel, as we talk about what matters to us.

"And the shepherds returned"—because, yes, they had to get back to work. As do we. They couldn't stay on that mountaintop where they'd seen the glory of God in full technicolor display, any more than we can keep it Christmas beyond the stroke of midnight tonight. But they came back different. They came back "glorifying and praising God for all they had heard and seen." Christmas marked the rest of their lives. God had made them forever worshipers and evangelists.

May He do the same with us.

MY PRAYER

O Lord, we praise You, we glorify You, we exalt You, we worship You! For to us has been born in Bethlehem a Savior, Christ the Lord—our Jesus, our hope of glory. Do something new and different in me, Lord, because of how You've spoken to me throughout this season. I seek You and surrender myself to You. I ask You to make me never the same—because of Christmas.

KEEP READING

— Psalm 51:10–17
"Open my lips, and my mouth will declare your praise" (v. 15)

— Isaiah 12:1–6
"Make known his deeds among the peoples" (v. 4)

— 2 Corinthians 3:12–18
"Where the Spirit of the Lord is, there is freedom" (v. 17)

MY RESPONSE

Try finding a worshipful, private moment at some point today where you can write out a prayer, expressing your desire to glorify Christ to all those around you. And remember, it's not about you and what you can do to serve Him. It's about Him—what *He* can do.

SIMEON'S SONG
"THE NUNC DIMITTIS"

He took him up in his arms and blessed God and said,

"Lord, now you are letting your servant depart in peace,
according to your word;
for my eyes have seen your salvation
that you have prepared in the presence of all peoples,
a light for revelation to the Gentiles,
and for glory to your people Israel."

(Luke 2:28–32)

PARTY OF ONE

Now there was a man in Jerusalem, whose name was Simeon,
and this man was righteous and devout, waiting for the
consolation of Israel, and the Holy Spirit was upon him.
(Luke 2:25)

How quickly our world moves on from Christmas. No sooner have we finally quieted ourselves inside our homes—stores closed, packages delivered, carols playing on an endless loop—than the ads and promos begin loudly inviting us to make our raucous plans for New Year. What could be next? Weight loss commercials?

That's why I'm drawn to spend another week here in the biblical songs of Christmas—drawn toward a character or two who don't show up as ceramic figures in our nativity scenes, yet who play key parts in rounding out what God was accomplishing through the gift of His Son to earth. Like Elizabeth and Mary and Zechariah and the shepherds, there's something different about these people—something we need to keep carrying with us as this year turns to next.

Simeon. He doesn't stand out by occupation or by his response to an angelic visitor, like some of the others we've seen. As far as we know, he was simply a layman, a worshiper of God, who lived in Jerusalem. But he was "righteous"—a keeper of the law, a man of upstanding character, fair and honest in his dealings with others. He was "devout"—a reverent follower of the Lord, pious and conscientious, one who desired to please God in every aspect of his life.

And he was "waiting"—something most of us find extremely hard to do. He was waiting for the Messiah. He was watching for God to act. He was concerned not only with himself and his own pedantic matters but with the people of his nation. His Spirit-led heart was marked by integrity, devotion, and a living, prayerful, faithful hope.

Those aren't easy things to live with, either today or in Simeon's day. But as we prepare to hear the song he shared with two unsettled parents and their barely month-old son, I ask you: If your bio sketch needed to be reduced to a single Luke 2:25 sentence—just over thirty words in this particular translation— what would you wish for it to say? And would its information make you as distinctive from the average after-Christmas man or woman in our culture (even our *Christian* subculture) as Simeon was in his day?

Most Jews of his time were going through the rituals, maybe doing righteous things, but not because they were truly righteous, not because they were truly devout, not because they were motivated to follow God by a deep-seated love for Him.

Simeon was different. And you and I can be different—willing to stand out for what might make us look a little crazy. Not because we're spiritually superior, but because we're looking and waiting for the only hope that's truly worth partying for.

MY PRAYER

Father, thank You for placing within Scripture those who struggled to obey You. Their stories give me confidence that You can work through my weakness. But thank You also for telling of those who inspire by their positive examples. May Your Spirit work in my heart so that He might grow in me righteousness, devotion, patience—faith, hope, love—in the name of Your Son.

———————◆———————

KEEP READING

— Numbers 14:21–24
"because he has a different spirit" (v. 24)

— Psalm 26:1–3
"Prove me, O Lord, and try me" (v. 2)

— Philippians 2:12–16
"among whom you shine as lights in the world" (v. 15)

———————◆———————

MY RESPONSE

How has a desire to be accepted and homogenized into culture hindered your relationship with Christ? What are the highest costs to pay for desiring to be different, for choosing only Him?

KEEP THE RECEIPT

He came in the Spirit into the temple, and when the parents brought in the child Jesus, to do for him according to the custom of the Law, he took him up in his arms and blessed God.
(Luke 2:27–28)

In one sense, salvation is something we seek and find. We come, we kneel, we reach out, we place our faith and belief in Jesus Christ. That's true. But in a deeper, much truer sense, salvation is something we receive. *God* comes—*He* reaches down—and gives us faith to believe on Him and in what He's done for us.

We *receive* Him more than we go out and *find* Him—not only in salvation, but throughout all of our lives.

In this prelude passage to the song of Simeon, we see both these facets in view. Presumably an old man by this time, he had been waiting many years to lay eyes on the Messiah. "It had been revealed to him by the Holy Spirit," the Bible says, "that he would not see death before he had seen the Lord's Christ" (Luke 2:26). So these scouting missions, like the one where he finally did find Jesus and His parents in the temple, were apparently part of Simeon's normal routine. He was habitually on the lookout—perhaps not knowing exactly what he was looking for, but trusting the Spirit to make the coordinates clear when the time and place were right for discovery.

The early church ascribed to Simeon the name *Theodoches*—"God receiver"—based on his reaction to the Christ child, as described in Luke 2:28, how he "took him up in his arms." He *received* Him. We don't know if he held the baby close and tight to his chest, the way you'd gather up a child in a smothering embrace. Perhaps by "up," the Scripture means he took Jesus from his mother and held him up with arms extended above his head, his eyes and worship pointed joyfully heavenward. The picture isn't painted to that level of detail.

All I know is that as I have meditated on this passage, I've found myself wanting to be more of a God-receiver. I make it my frequent prayer to Him, asking Him to help me receive Christ today with greater joy, greater faith, greater humility. I want to say and mean it with all my heart—fully satisfied in Him, fully contented in Him—"Lord, it is enough to me that I have Christ. I am His, and He is mine."

As long as you and I are here in these bodies, we will never escape the experience of living with longings and desires, waiting for things to happen and change. But I believe God's way of navigating us through longings unfulfilled is to teach us how to keep receiving Him each day, just as we received Him initially. May we never stop being a *Theodoches*, no matter how old or tired our waiting eyes become.

Reach out to Him—yes, reach out—but in reaching, *receive* . . .

MY PRAYER

Better than anyone, Lord, You understand the unmet longings of my heart. You also know the time and place when those longings You desire to fulfill here on earth will reach fruition. But even if they must wait until I am face to face with You in glory, may I be satisfied today—and all the days in between—with the sufficiency of Your presence in the face of Jesus.

KEEP READING

— Psalm 24:3–6
"He will receive blessing from the LORD" (v. 5)

— Isaiah 40:1–2
"Comfort, comfort my people, says your God" (v. 1)

— Colossians 2:6–7
"As you received Christ Jesus the Lord, so walk in him" (v. 6)

MY RESPONSE

What would "receiving Christ" look like as you work through the coming day? What are some of the thoughts and fears He could conquer if you set your mind toward being a God-receiver?

MATTERS OF LIFE AND DEATH

*"Lord, now you are letting your servant depart in peace,
according to your word."*
(Luke 2:29)

Nunc Dimittis. This is the traditional title given to Simeon's song, again derived from the Latin rendering of its opening words: "Now You let depart."

Simeon was saying he could die now. The Lord had done what He had promised. Simeon, having seen his Savior, could now see death in a whole new light. He was ready, he said, to "depart in peace."

Departing, in the original Greek, carried the idea of being released from an assignment, dismissed as a servant. It meant you'd done your job. You'd fulfilled your duty. You were loosed from your responsibility. Free to go. But people of that day applied this word to a number of different contexts, each of which gives insight into how a believer in Christ should be able to think about death because of his or her relationship with Him.

To "depart" was sometimes used in speaking of a prisoner released from his chains, set free from captivity. *Isn't that what happens when a child of God dies?* We're released from bondage to sin and this sinful world, released from broken bodies that hinder the freedom we feel inside.

It was also used as a nautical metaphor, referring to a ship being untied from its mooring. *Isn't that what happens when a child of God dies?* Having been held fast in place, we feel the rope slacken and fall away, freeing us to head toward our desired destination.

Beyond even these meanings, it also contained a military connection. When armies broke camp to move on to their next station or deployment, they were said to be departing. *Isn't this, too, what happens when a child of God dies?* Paul compared our earthly bodies to a "tent" (2 Cor. 5:1–4), awaiting a permanent structure.

I mention all of this, not to glorify death (of course), but to affirm that for a believer, death is no monster to be feared. Despite feeling the normal human emotions of sadness and separation, we have no need to cling ferociously to life on this earth. Death is release, freedom, passage, home. To live in true reality, for a Christian, is to live with an eagerness and expectancy of finally uniting with Him.

Donald Cargill, a Scotsman martyred for his faith in 1681, delivered a long, impassioned message from the steps of the scaffold where he would soon be hanged and beheaded. He called this day "the sweetest and most glorious day that ever did my eyes see. Farewell reading and preaching, praying and believing. Farewell wanderings, reproaches, and sufferings. Welcome joy unspeakable and full of glory."

That's what I sense in Simeon's song as well, a freedom entirely dependent on that baby in his arms. The One whose birth we've celebrated this season is both our means of life and our liberation in death.

MY PRAYER

Thank You, Lord, that our eyes have seen Your salvation, that You've made Christ known to us. Thank You for the promised hope of fellowship with You in heaven, and how awareness of Your eternal provision reflects back into my life today. Because You've opened my heart to welcome You, I can welcome each part of my journey now with faith and confidence. Thank You, Lord!

———————◆———————

KEEP READING

— Job 19:23–27
"For I know that my Redeemer lives" (v. 25)

— Psalm 23:1–6
"And I shall dwell in the house of the LORD forever" (v. 6)

— 2 Timothy 4:6–8
"I have finished the race, I have kept the faith" (v. 7)

———————◆———————

MY RESPONSE

The biggest challenge you're facing right now may not be death. But how can the certainty of life forever with Jesus impact the way you approach your current difficulties each day?

DO YOU HEAR WHAT I HEAR?

*"For my eyes have seen your salvation that you have prepared
in the presence of all peoples, a light for revelation to the
Gentiles, and for glory to your people Israel."*
(Luke 2:30–32)

oo many of us, I'm afraid, when reading some of the more familiar Scriptures, would admit we sometimes bypass the wonder. We hear the words; we miss what's really there. But in certain cases, what's missing is not so much wonder but *shock*. Our distance from the times and traditions when these things were originally being said can prevent us from noticing at first glance (especially *hundredth* glance) just how shocking some of these statements really were—and are.

So picture Simeon with me for a moment in the temple, standing in the part of the sanctuary where only Jews could enter. In fact, a marble screen, four-and-a-half feet high, was positioned at the bottom of the steps leading up to this area, warning all

Gentiles "on pain of death" not to venture beyond the court where their kind was allowed to mingle. Those *Gentiles*. (Hear the disdain in that italics.) Uncircumcised, unclean, pagan, heathen. The Jews considered them rejects, completely outside God's inner circle.

Now return your gaze back up into the temple, beyond the first level, the highly active court of the women. Climb another fifteen steps higher to an arched gate leading into the court of Israel. Here, at this gate, is where Jewish parents would bring their forty-day-old infant sons, along with an offering for the purification of the mother following childbirth. By this point, you're far removed from the much lower court of the Gentiles. You're deep into the fabric of Jewish culture now. You can see it, feel it, hear it, smell it burning from the altars.

Somewhere in the midst of this noise and bustle is where the Spirit alerted Simeon that the Messiah was *right there*, in that woman's arms—the One he'd been waiting his whole life to see. And in beholding Him, Simeon made a statement that few if any of those around him ever expected to come out of someone's mouth in that holy place. Not only did he dare to speak of salvation as God's design for "all peoples," but he mentioned the Gentiles first, ahead of his own people Israel.

Shocking!

The reason our jaws don't drop is because we've had two thousand New Testament years of growing accustomed to it. The reason their jaws *shouldn't* have dropped is because God had been dropping hints of it throughout the ages, through all the prophets they knew so well. But as you read Simeon's words again yourself, leave room for your own heart to expand now in grateful worship. "For God, who said, 'Let light shine out of darkness,' has shone in our hearts to give the light of the knowledge of the glory of God in the face of Jesus Christ" (2 Cor. 4:6).

Shockingly wonderful.

MY PRAYER

Fill me with wonder again, Lord, at both the brilliance and mercy of Your salvation. Shock me at what You have done. Awaken my wooden imagination so I can see with fresh, spiritual eyes. The privilege You've given me, enabling me to stand redeemed in Your presence, is a miracle of the highest order. May the wonder of it—of Christmas—shock me into a new year of revival.

KEEP READING

— Psalm 98:1–3
"The LORD has made known his salvation" (v. 2)

— Isaiah 52:7–10
"And all the ends of the earth shall see the salvation of our God" (v. 10)

— 1 Timothy 2:5–7
"There is one mediator between God and men, the man Christ Jesus" (v. 5)

MY RESPONSE

What adjustments could you make to your own Bible reading and study that would increase your awareness of wonder—even shock!—at what the inspired words of Scripture are actually saying?

IT HURTS TO TELL YOU

"Behold, this child is appointed for the fall and rising of many in Israel, and for a sign that is opposed (and a sword will pierce through your own soul also), so that thoughts from many hearts may be revealed."
(Luke 2:34–35)

Blessing is often accompanied with pain. Being a parent, for example. Few things can rival the blessing of welcoming a child into your life, your home, your family. But who else besides a parent—a mother, perhaps, in particular—knows the depths of human pain? Oh, how the blessing is shot through with anguish when that child you love more than you love yourself is suffering in ways you cannot prevent or fix.

Simeon's closing words to Mary and Joseph, fresh on the heels of such encouraging blessing, cast a painful, lengthening shadow that, of course, was specifically true of what they and their baby would come to experience. But as we know, the shadow has never stopped falling. This gospel that we believe, as glorious as are its benefits, is no bed of roses. We, too, experience our own taste of persecution, suffering, struggle, and conflict.

But what Simeon said cuts deeper than even that. Mary, we know, would go on to see her son rejected, reviled, misunderstood, and openly abused, to the point of being gruesomely tortured and murdered. She was there. She saw it all. This sword that Simeon had talked about—a large, broad, double-edged sword, piercing her soul not just once but again and again—yes, she would feel the stabbing fulfillment of that prophecy.

But of all the pain that would course through her nerve endings throughout the course of her life, imagine the pain that congealed around this one thought: It was *her* sin, not only that of those self-righteous Pharisees and those cruel Roman executioners, that put her precious son through such agony on that cross. As one who was inclined toward "pondering" things "in her heart" (Luke 2:19), what wracking of pain do you think she felt when she pondered how much of that blood was on His own mother's hands?

The greater we love Him and the deeper we know His truth, the more that sword of responsibility should turn in our bodies. It should wake us every day with renewed determination (as Luke 9:23 says) to deny ourselves, take up our cross, and follow Him. Greater still, the more acutely the pain motivates us—the closer we draw to Jesus—the more our hearts should break at the lostness of the world around us, including the deadness and despair that runs much too deeply in the family of God, even in ourselves.

Pain is to be expected. The pain comes with the blessing.

Thank God, of course, the Son paid the price for it because of His great love for both us and the Father. Thank God, He gives more grace than the pain can ever dish out. But don't run from the pain, as if the gospel didn't require it. Let it draw you up into greater passion for Him who one day will deliver us from all of it.

MY PRAYER

How do I begin to thank You, Lord, for enduring such pain, for bearing my sin without anger toward me? I bow before You today because of the heartache I feel for causing You to suffer. And yet You invite me to lift up my eyes, giving me grace to endure not only this hurt but every painful thing You allow into my life. I trust You to keep me, and I love You for loving me.

◆

KEEP READING

— Psalm 38:17–22
"My pain is ever before me" (v. 17)

— Jeremiah 15:16–20
"Why is my pain unceasing, my wound incurable?" (v. 18)

— Romans 9:1–5
"I have great sorrow and unceasing anguish in my heart" (v. 2)

◆

MY RESPONSE

Spiritually speaking, what is the difference between avoiding pain and embracing pain? How can you let the pain that comes with blessing become a deeper invitation into the heart of God?

SONG SHARING

There was a prophetess, Anna . . . and coming up at that very hour she began to give thanks to God and to speak of him to all who were waiting for the redemption of Israel.
(Luke 2:36, 38)

he biblical songs of Christmas. They're not exactly ones that leave you humming along, and yet . . . it doesn't mean they easily leave you.

Elizabeth's Song, such an exciting start, remember? Sheer joy never sounds more beautiful than when coming from the heart of an older woman who refuses to let life dim her expectation. Mary's Song, a reminder never to discount the maturity to be found in the younger generation. Zechariah's Song, showing that underneath the hesitant and reticent are some of God's most expressive, articulate worshipers. The Angels' Song, glory of glories. And finally, Simeon's Song, a fitting close, bridging the wonder of Christmas with the responsibilities and stewardship such a gift entails into the future.

And here we stand, together in the midst of that future, as well as on the precipice of a freshly numbered version of it. A new slate of days stretches out before us, both inviting and daring us to do some things differently this year, with what God has done in our hearts this Christmas.

That's why I'd like to end on a biblical note of response—the response embodied by an elderly widow who was also present in the temple on that day when Mary and Joseph showed up there with . . . with Anna's Savior . . . with Jesus.

Anna: worshiper and witness.

Worshiper. "She began to give thanks to God." She loved Him so much that even though her own marriage had ended with her husband's death only seven years into their relationship, she'd purposed to give herself fully to the Lord for the remainder of her long life. "She did not depart from the temple, worshiping with fasting and prayer night and day" (Luke 2:37). So her instant reflex upon realizing the identity of the Christ child was immediate praise. Praise and—

Witness. Anna, like Simeon, and like others in probably a small-numbered remnant of God's people, was among what I call "the fellowship of the waiting." She kept the coal of her heart close to the coals of others whose lives burned for God's visitation. And from the fire set ablaze by their faith and unity, she could not keep to herself the tidings of what the Lord was doing. From her faithfully prayerful posture arose an uncontainable urge to share with others what she'd seen.

I believe these two watchwords are appropriate ones to carry with us into a new year. Life is our great opportunity both to *worship* and *witness*.

Keep singing, keep sharing the songs of Christmas.

MY PRAYER

Thank You, Lord, for ministering so personally to me this Christmas. Thank You for throwing wide the window on Your mercy and power, evoking from me a fresh intensity of worship. And as You carry me into the new year tomorrow, help me enter it with a song on my lips— the song of Your salvation, more precious to me than ever, and eagerly shared at every opportunity.

KEEP READING

— Psalm 71:15–18
"I still proclaim your wondrous deeds" (v. 17)

— Zephaniah 3:9–13
"They shall seek refuge in the name of the LORD" (v. 12)

— Matthew 28:16–20
"And when they saw him they worshiped him" (v.17)

MY RESPONSE

What if you aligned your hopes for the new year around these two words—worship and witness? Into what practical directions could they take your prayerful plans?

Revive Our Hearts™

Through its various outreaches and the teaching ministry of Nancy DeMoss Wolgemuth, *Revive Our Hearts* is calling women around the world to freedom, fullness, and fruitfulness in Christ.

Offering sound, biblical teaching and encouragement for women through . . .

Books & Resources Nancy's books, True Woman Books, and a wide range of audio/video

Broadcasting Two daily, nationally syndicated broadcasts (*Revive Our Hearts* and *Seeking Him*) reaching over one million listeners a week

Events & Training True Woman Conferences and events designed to equip women's ministry leaders and pastors' wives

Internet ReviveOurHearts.com, TrueWoman.com, and LiesYoungWomenBelieve.com; daily blogs, and a large, searchable collection of electronic resources for women in every season of life

Believing God for a grassroots movement of authentic revival and biblical womanhood . . .

Encouraging women to:

- Discover and embrace God's design and mission for their lives.
- Reflect the beauty and heart of Jesus Christ to their world.
- Intentionally pass on the baton of truth to the next generation.
- Pray earnestly for an outpouring of God's Spirit in their families, churches, nation, and world.

Visit us at **ReviveOurHearts.com.** We'd love to hear from you!